Give me a reason to smile and laugh
give me a reason to smile beyound
to smile so wide my cheeks burn in joy
pain
things that i wish for, for the things
ll come through. Can i smile for the
my art for the happiness in ink, on
ly on the page, on the walls that pro-
ect my spirit. It isn't that hard
Just give me love

In Search Of Magick

By Samantha Nicole Traina

This book is dedicated to my family
who gave me the space to explore when I was lost,
break down when it became too much,
and showed me the possibilities that
the universe has to offer.

Thank You.

Table Of Contents

Table Of Contents

Table Of Contents

A Touch Of Magick

A touch of magick
I felt it the first time
in the dead winter at night
with dim, beautiful,
twinkling lights.

It started under my bones,
radiated outward,
consumed me whole
till a smile ripped apart my lips
and I broke out into a confusing laughing fit.

I don't know how to conjure it.
No drug or substance is the same fix.
I'll never pretend to understand
a rush some might get
from the chemicals
our brain can't forget,

but a touch of magick
I felt it again
from the graze of lips
slotted together
the perfect fit.

I felt it crossing under a bridge
to a city of winter and wind,
marveling at a frozen
lake Michigan
so close to where I would soon live.

I felt it driving,
escaping to the west as fast as I could
fleeing the feeling
of being always misunderstood.

I felt it when words fly
perfectly onto pages
while they flit dangerous close
with my mind forgetting their place.

I felt it when the wind
would gather up:
gray clouds, lightening, thunder,
all that energy circling
as if it is almost stuck.

I felt it moving between
headstones and pine trees
My sister and I exploring
a deadly feeling of ease.

I felt it
a touch of magick
with a candle flame
twisting and flexing
so close to immeasurable pain.

I feel it now
writing this down.
A connection
I have found
a feeling indescribable
and unbound.

In Search Of Magick

A touch of magick
forever in search of
and perhaps
always found.

Sun Met The Moon

I did a spell
as the sun met the moon
clouded over for a second,
hidden, yet never consumed.

I wished for us to meet and
for the death of all my worries to be complete.
Everyone else seemed to fade away
as the black candle flickered,
I thought maybe it would be okay.

"Hi, I'm here.
I'm ready to begin.
Wherever you are
feel my energy on your skin.
 It is time for our loneliness to end."

The black candle fell,
yet there was no black wax
left over from the spell.

Does that mean you didn't hear me?
It has been three years since then.
I still keep looking for you
just around the bend.

All the others left
at the end of the eclipse.
Anxiety over took them.
I think that was part of my intended wish.

But what real power
do I actually have?
What could I draw
from the moon leaving the sun?
Maybe nothing happened.
Maybe it has just begun.

I did a spell
as the sun met the moon.
I keep trust that it worked
that I'll be meeting you soon.

Half Way

I don't wanna be here anymore
sleeping on the garden floor.
What is all of this for?

If not for excitement,
if not for despair,
why be stuck in the middle
clenching my fingers
holding on to my cares?

Emptiness:
unsolvable riddle
unreachable door.
None of this matters,
at least not anymore.

I lay at the crossroads
hoping for a sign.
Is halfway far enough?
Will I ever cross the finish line?

I Thought There Would Be Fire

I thought there would be fire
hidden in my blood,
yet the stars are saying
there is absolutely none.

There is enough air
with windy gusts a storms must.
The earth over powers it
refusing to bust.

The smallest drop of water
makes me wonder if that is why
it is what I crave.
Day in and day out
parched with every word that I say.

I thought there would be fire
hidden in my bones.
I have felt all that passion building up
carrying me forward
even when I'm alone.
Yet there is none to be found
in what the stars foretold

There was air to carve them,
earth to make their structure strong,
water as the blood inside the,
no fire to belong.

I thought there would be fire
hidden in my soul.
After all that is where all the creation grows
from sparks and passions
so where did it go?
How can it not be there
when I swear I smell the smoke?

As I Will It

As I will it,
but my will seems fragile
prone to breaking,
changing,
rearranging itself into something
I never wanted.

As I will it,
but my will is unstable
a ground I stand on
trembling like my lips,
nervous to let my disagreements slip.

As I will it,
but my will is not always faithful;
quick to jump ship
to something new or better backed
with evidence
presented by those with better confidence.

As I will it,
but my will likes disguises
appearing like it came from me,
my experience,
when really it was whispered to me
because someone else liked it.

As I will it,
but my will is hesitant
trailing off to a drop off...
Will the universe question
am I competent?

As I will it,
but is my will enough
to pull creation
to create my salvation
refine my diamond in the rough?

As I will it,
but my will holds doubts;
small tricky things
hard to pin down
and always wandering about.

As I will it
sometimes I want to shout
as I watch my will
take me along
a whole new route.

I Want The Thrill

I have to wonder how many have settled before;
how many were wronged for too long
and now the crave a simple song?

How many of them will pity me
as I linger and wait simply?
My soul once exploded
gave me shivers down my spine.
Since then I have craved the feeling.
I'll chase it till I've run out of time:

euphoric joy as I create,
holding it in as I cross the city gate,
a breath of caffeine lingering taste,
your marks on my skin yet to dissipate.

I want that thrill
air caught in my lungs until
relief sweeps in electric fill.

Rip my smile wide
ignoring the ache in my sides.
Energy: ever changing tide,
I savor it as I realize
it always will slip out of reach.
I find only anxiety where so many find peace.

I wonder how many have settled before.
I wonder if I'll feel satisfied when death
knocks on my door.

As Simple Sip

A simple sip and a breath.
Have I made magick from this?

A habit repeated for years.
An association of peace, of pause
between never ending noise.

They don't expect you to speak back
with a rim of something delicious
between your lips.
Taste on the tongue
down the throat
as calming as the perfect song.

Have I made magick from this?

At some point they now
associate it with me:
A hot cup of something wonderful
Early morning
Pause
Sip
Now you may speak.

Those moments of peace
come with such ease.
Maybe an international knowing
that we all need to breathe
with sips in between,

but have I made magick from this?
A now almost unconscious knowing
as my shoulders drop from the smell,
I curl the warmth of the mug to my chest,
my fingers cease their taping,
and anger seeps out of my bones
finally, I can rest.

A simple sip and breath:
I make magick with this.

In The Dust

Oh my my my
this crossroads has me terrified.

The wind gathers up
can I hang tough?
Will you move for what:
love, trust, pixie dust?
Moon too full or too dark?
I can't see it anyway.
I'm waiting for that spark.

Move, I scream
MOVE
or your going to lose it all.
Backtracking isn't as bad
as taking that trust fall.

Dust
is in my lungs.
It coats everything I touch
a reminder I don't belong.
I use to love storms,
but this one seems wrong

Dust in the wind,
rust on the mountain,
the rain stops half way down
like a broken fountain.

Staring up I'm stuck
like the rain caught
in the middle of the sky.
Dust swirls around me.
I brought myself here,
yet for the life of me
I can not remember why.

Make Believe

Can't you see?
This maze is all just make believe.
Follow me
into light mosaic distortion
fixing into combustion.

Let it scatter,
let life take you over,
be what needs to fall part
for your new start.
This maze is all make believe.
Your dream,
this feeling of the tide
falling
away.

This maze is make believe.
Come play with me.
Let's run through
the oddest geometry.
Come away with me.
Let chaos of the heart
run free
'cause this is all
just a maze of make believe.

It is screaming

"This is a trick
you won't find a fix
all of that good
you'll quickly forget.
The dark isn't your friend
remember the fiend instead,
always caution
ignore the voices in your head!"

I hear your advice.
I have taken heed
but perhaps caution
isn't what I need.

Demons have whispered
longer than in witchcraft
I have lingered.
Worries from parents,
grandparents, friends.
A different worry
screams instead.

"What if you miss it?
What if the hope
at the bottom of the box is lost?
What if you walk
past a piece of yourself
too afraid of the cost?"

A different voice whispers
deep deep within,
Yet louder than the hesitance.
"Fucking jump in!
Your hesitance
could be joy missed!"

Terrified of experience,
of the words they will hiss.

"Fuck that nonsense,"
that quiet voice now screams.

"Fuck over thinking!
Just go dive in,
envelope, engulf, expand!
Caution they will grant you
when you dare to take
your own hand."

Nostalgia Drug

Nostalgia
is like a fucking drug,
reminding you of the things you once did love
and still do
and when the moment strikes you
it pulls you back in
to all the things
you so confidently once abandoned.

I left because of you
and bad memories.
I left because no one else was there,
no connection
just a bunch of irregularities.

I searched again and again
for a place like that,
where I would cross the line
and breath in the electric
feel that would set me alive.
Was it only time?
A congregation of memories,
bad and good, all stirred up
into a singular vibe?

Why was that home?
Why was it there I could grow?
Will I ever feel that again ...

or will I always feel slightly off and
maybe a bit broken
to not be in the city that is my birthplace?
Is it only there I can feel safe?

Will it always hold my blood and soul
regardless of how far the divide
or is it just this simple moment in time?

If I stay here long enough,
linger through streets and bars,
collect a few moments and broken hearts,
laugh and cry and wander when I'm frustrated,
will this horrible feeling become abated?

Will the nostalgia switch the location
of its never ending hold?
Will I be able to finally call
this place I so craved
home.

So I Can Breathe

I haven't felt cold in oh so long.
It is nostalgia,
something about ya,
feeling that chill come along.

It enters your bones
makes you sink into covers
like a heavy stone.
Still that shiver continues to grow.

I used to despise when
winter would arrive,
feeling all this death
like everything good left
had retreated inside.

Yet now I crave
the coldest of days
rain frozen and frosted
for me to run in and play.

Please ignore the sun,
stay a little longer,
every goose-bump
makes my soul a little stronger.

Change the leaves,
capture the breeze,
whatever you need

I will beg please!
Just stay on my skin
and enter my lungs
so I can finally breathe.

The Things I Find

I like to find the things
that set the spark:
songs, movies, books,
any piece of art,

but it must capture my attention,
jerk me out of my robotic state,
entrap my fascination,
all wonders shoved directly in my face.

Old loves keep me excited,
but they must always be invited.
I push myself to re-consume
the love and awe, let it re-bloom.

I know the simple things matter most.
To them I would give all my toasts,
but those simple things
are on a trail to something more.
They seem to be bread crumbs
I wonder what they have in store.

Where will they lead me?
Can I devour them whole?
Is it something else that will complete me?
Is it remembering this is all a journey
the only real goal?

I like to find things
that start a spark.
Maybe it is my whole life
that is my favorite piece of art.

The Maiden

Why must the maiden be naive?
Maybe she was just doing as she pleased
wandering into the seas
of green leaves and then a pit of black.
Loved or attacked?
Hiding or fighting her way back?

Why must the maiden be naive?
How is it that what tricked her
was a seed;
the very things her and her mother rule over completely?
Such assumption for the reason of her consumption
over simplifying what she did need.

Why must the maiden choose between
sovereignty and family?
I wonder if she ate the seed
with much more clarity;
refusing to obey mother, father, or husband
entirely.
Some might call it a maiden's greed
to want life and death
together
for the rest of eternity;
float between the two
and bringing change with her
happily.

Why must the maiden be naive?
When a nymph attempts to woo what is hers
suddenly it is jealousy.
Why plead for the lovers release?
unless she knew their feelings with every heartbeat.

Why must the maiden be naive?
Maybe just maybe,
she savored the taste of every seed
with a smirk allowing us the joy
to believe whatever
we wanted to believe.

Haunt Me

I wish it didn't still haunt me
that feeling of summer time winds,
feeling the energy, needles, and pins
all up and down my skin.

The look of his smile as we ran around town
too busy to worry about it all burning down.

I wish I knew what to say
when all their skin was littered with red.
Always just a phone call away
I got to use to the dead.
Another damn tragedy
waiting for me, shaking its head.

Still I believed
I could make it out
with my dreams alive.
Just kept faith,
push for us all to survive
and then it was nothing but
sad when I realized

I was all on my own.

I wish it didn't still haunt me
that feeling of fall time winds
and the look on her face
when the death toll would begin.

Bit by bit
we all would sell our souls
for anything that would keep us afloat,
including the ties that bind us
and now I'm always alone.

I still say those three little words,
but the last time I meant them was July 21st
of 2013 and they never were returned.

Did I even really mean them or was it make believe?
I remember that pit in my chest
expanding as you explained
how little you should have meant to me.

I wish it didn't still haunt me
that feeling of the spring time winds.
Pacing back and forth
in different cities, trying again
wondering what am I to do;
all of these feeling the most
frustrating muse.

Is that why they all say
those are our best days?
Not because of good ol' times
or that the bad memories fade,
but 'cause it's the only time
you actually truly feel alive
in between the suffering,
just trying to survive.

Yeah, I swear life is better:
death hasn't called for a while and I've lost all their letters
and I don't feel nearly as broken as I used to,
but I would be lying if I said I didn't miss you

and the way you all said my name,
with trust in your eyes and so much pain,
like the whole damn world was playing its own sick game.
We were all just along for the ride,
trying our hardest to not feel so dead inside.

I wish it didn't still haunt me
the feeling of winter winds,
when I never did actually fit in.
These ghosts never put me
at the top of their mind,
yet in so many moments
they are at the top of mine.

Like the one I dragged between my legs,
to the one who put his fingers around my neck,
to the one who pretended it never really happened,
to the one who couldn't live another day
to the one who loved me like sister, then call me a bitch and
cast me away
to the ones who followed because them I betrayed
and I hated myself a little more each day.

To the one who found her dreams
and couldn't see they might drown me.
To the one who actually gave me hope,
but really only ever saw me as a childish joke ...
and all the ones who forgot me in the end.

They all have me wishing it didn't still haunt me:
that feeling on the edge of the winds.
All that energy feels like needles and pins
all up and down my skin,
as Hope
starts stubbornly
creeping its way back in.

Things I Feared

I used to ignore the things I feared
horror stories real and fiction.
I saw no reason for consumption
and I always steered clear.

The news was a useless tool
even though I knew ignorance
might make me a fool,
but the happiness
I found in my world
allowed me to ignore
everything so cruel.

Still fascinated
when stories would leak in.
Dark colors to stories to statistics
down the rabbit hole I would spin
only to become too afraid once again.

I don't know why
my fear seemed to step aside.
Maybe it is just biding its time,
waiting to clutch my heart
and force me to run and hide,

but for now I am intrigued
by the dark things.
Ignore them? Oh how I try,
but then the bell rings
I become that silly cat
amazed that they forgot the line
of satisfaction bringing it back.

Why is knowledge
always so vilified?
As if us, the silly masses,
can't seem to handle
the state of being satisfied.

I realize how on edge I was
before exploring the dark,
Now I explore it just 'cause
no major journey to embark.
Answers are not where I find the mark.

I enjoy peeling back
the layers of the things I fear,
revealing pieces of myself
now seeing them so clear.

Perhaps

Perhaps there is nothing.
Perhaps this is all in my head.
Perhaps there is more.
Perhaps it started with a bang
at the will of something greater
than ever existed before.

Perhaps we are all just waiting to come alive
longing for something to compare our stride.
Perhaps we will all reach the level we deem deity
that's why we hear their whispers;
each life a lesson in brevity.

Perhaps we wouldn't recognize
ourselves across dimensional lines.
Perhaps our dreams in day and night
blur the lines enough to see the light.

Perhaps each creation is our practice
learning to determine what fact is.
Perhaps this is all nonsense
a stride into the ridiculous.

Perhaps I won't know
until the light fades from my eyes,
but for now it is fun to wonder
perhaps this is right.

The Hell Inside Myself

I took a trip to the Hell inside myself.

It felt like spilling past
pieces of broken glass:
stabbing,
non-stop healing,
for once finally seeing
the demons that grinned
at the site of me.
Instead of cowering
I smiled back respectively.

I cried at their claws,
shivered at the evidence
of my own flaws.

They give me shields
and blades to defend
against those that
my despair would commend.
So I didn't fight or attack.
I stood with arms open to them,
watched as love appeared where it
once was only in lack.

Claws, teeth, and sharp demon eyes
morphed into me, showing me truths
revealing all the lies.

I came back from the Hell within myself.
I remember it fondly. I feel them still moving
those shadows of stealth.

Quietly,
whispers almost silently
a love undying to confide in me.
This promise
Spoken with demonic ferocity:
love shown to all parts of me entirely,
protected evermore
from the hatred in outward society.
Barrier kept strong even if
spoken perhaps impolitely.

If others ever dare
to question my worth and gravity
back to the Hell within myself
I will venture happily.

The Veil Is Thin

The veil is thin
all without and within
easy to reach
graze the skin.
The dead,
the gone,
the parts they don't belong
connected to where we live.

The veil is thin and I reach out
to parts I constantly think about
other realms and beings
and versions of me
taking another route.

The veil is thin
and dark seeps in
revealing shadows
and grays where light can't always
cast away.

The veil is thin
between now and then.
What's to come?
May I please tap in
to what I might be given?

The veil is thin
and whispers call sweetly
to lure me
to something I could love or hate
contently.

The veil is thin
a new beginning
has come again.
My gratitude
to those I have journeyed with
solitude to honor them with a gift.

The veil is thin
bless the universe and the gifts it has given.
I reach out to clasp
what might be reaching back.

The veil is thin but as it grows
I wonder what will be taken?
What will become ash and dust,
crumble to make room?
What will withstand the rust?

The veil is thin
on Samhain.
What will you do with
what you have been given?

Revisit History

It was like revisiting history
and old patterns came on so easily.
You even looked like him:
the shape of your nose
and lips were so similar.

So I wonder if I need a reminder
of what that spark felt like
before I can fall again
and forget all that strife.

Yet, how quickly you annoy me!
How fast this feeling is spoiling,
turned rotten and wrong,
quickly feeling like I don't belong.

It is too much the same?
Too many red flags to play this game.
I'm done; out before we even
had time to walk about,

but revisiting that misery
reminded me of the pleasure
lost in forgotten history.
I don't want the same,
but I wouldn't mind
if that feeling would come again.

Who I am?

When I think of who I am
at my center my core
there is a girl standing barefoot
at the center of the storm.

Her hair is darker
Then the clouds rolling in
lips pale
holding a barely detectable grin.

Wind whips her locks around her face.
Arms open wide to the sky
a loving embrace.

When I think of who I am at my core
it's toes digging into dirt on the forest floor.
It's golden brown eyes
that have seen thousands of suns set and rise,
coming alive as lightning streaks across the sky.

Who I am at my core
is the wind gathering up
before the rain slams it
in the downpour.
On my face a single drop
clearing away the dirt and muck.

Who is she at my core?
Listening intently to branches
creak before
the whole world seems
to opens its sky.
The rain washes away
and brings hellos and goodbyes.

Who am I at my core
is that terrifying energy
within the calm before the storm.

People Like Us

It's all earth dry, wind, grit
pink orange skies; red rust liquid lies
escape up high
never actually satisfied.

Maybe this dry sunbathing air
will wick away all my
aggravation, worries, and cares?
Why was it here
that I now feel the need,
to venture outside
listen to the wind through the trees?

The thunder rolls in
monsoon level winds;
the only time when I can laugh,
but then feel abandoned.

I remember walking between
sky-scrappers tunnel streams.
Oh, how that wind
always made me feel alive again,

but now it's dust
clouding up my heart with
a list of musts.
I can't see past
never feeling good enough.
I've lost all passion,
forgotten the feeling of lust.
Even the universe
has lost my trust.

So I sit here,
with all this earth, sand, and dust
hoping whatever is out there
hasn't forgotten people like us.

Something To Hide

Something else to hide
I'll break it open wide.
The truth may be cold,
but I'll be warmer on the inside.

Impending trouble around the bend.
Time makes this weight crushing
another lie you will defend.
You always think it is so well hidden.

Foundations are troubled with
truth growing in the cracks.
Last?
Please
I'd rather be cast out into the sea
then ever drown in the misery
of your company.

I can't keep holding you up.
I'm never going to be strong enough.
I have my own demons
dear old friends of mine.
Please don't give me something else to hide.
They'll break it open wide.
Truth will chill you to the bone,
but I'll be warmer on the inside.

Loki's Game

Do you wanna play a game?
Do you want to run the maze?
Can you stand on your own two feet?
Can you find something worth playing for?

This game is fun
Can you trust me?
Take my hand ...
Will I let you fall?
Can you catch yourself?

Wanna play a game?

Wanna have some fun?
Wanna get in the mud,
the dirt, and the grind?

Wanna Play a Game?

Why are you so scared?
What is terrifying?
What is it about this mischief and this lie that scares you?

Can't you handle yourself?
Can you stand on your own two feet?
Can't you pick yourself back up
with your own magick and beliefs?

Wanna Play a Game?

Give to me the most sacred parts of yourself
and trust you can not trust what I will do with it.

Wanna Play a game?
Wanna wait in the darkness and
see what is there in the sensual playful ground ...

Can't you stand on your own two feet?
Figure it out.
Adapt.

Wanna Play a Game?

Self Love Spell

With these words I pass along
a spell of sorts I know to be strong
as the knowing in my bones
that love of self, even in darkest of shadows,
forever grows.

Interact if you wish
or skim right past and nothing will stick.
This is a just a Hand
reaching out
in case the doubt
is creeping in
that universe and all around
have only taken
your comfort, your confidence,
left you feeling broken.

Feel this in the cracks of every break
my energy passed to you
of which you are free to take.
This is just the water to the seed
of self love I know there to be
buried always deep.

I know of demons.
I have greeted and loved mine,
but if you'd rather destroy yours that is more than fine.
Nothing is greater than what
always lies beneath
the trials and the struggles
that face You and Me.

Feel it in whatever shape you please
a bit of energy guided by technology
with simple ease
or just sit and take it in
every word I have written.

I feel the love in my veins,
bones, and soul.
There is more than enough and
still it continues to grow
even as doubts,
suggestions, and insecurities try
the overflow
will drown them alive.

This energy I pass on to you
love of light or of shadow
or both if you choose.

As I will it
It will be.

Re-fractured Soul Bones

Re-fracture my soul bones
still in the dark.
I will overcome
sinking swamps and old nostalgia
erase their lingering mark.

Allow in the creep
down into the sinking
feeling of blood, dirt, and healing.

Death always seemed so sweet.
Old, nature and moss, instinct
irises black zoned out
reasons to live we long
forgot about.

We break them
to make it heal right.
The pain leading to more
then the fire behind our eyes.

Re-fractured soul bones
held together tight
by our will to live
not just survive.

Oh Chaos...

I never thought I could love Chaos
the greater lesson life had taught
All my life running to so few
I didn't respect what you were trying to do.

I learned to love something more:
the changing of open doors.

"That's how hearts beat darling! That's how life get started.
That's how life ends.
Chaos is more than we can truly comprehend."

Back bending please explain
I'm dying for you.
Chaos is running through my veins.

Did we make it
through storms,
lighting strikes,
fears in headlights?

I am wide eyed for you
pieces broken down
lost and never found.
The feelings I had for you
becoming a burning need to drown.

Gods damn it,
it's in my veins now!
Within that chaos
a purpose found.

I Need Armour

Sometimes I need armour.
Black cascading confidence
bidding insecurities
good riddance.

Each pieces blessed once before
cloaking me in sovereignty
as I walk out the door.

A bit magick
in simple fabric
and in my inner power
I am suddenly sure, confident.

I cultivate
all things that help me create
someone who reaches for joy
and does not hesitate.

I'd Rather Watch The Smoke

Why must I entertain
half-ass horrible conversation?
More like slow
deliberate
frustrations,

I'd rather stay in tonight
and watch the smoke rise high,
diluting in the night sky.

It's too many cups overflowing
emotions controlling
resist a fight
I'd rather burn the herbs
and let the anger simmer
at the sight.

I can't even see the moon.
Is it against me too?
Maybe, but for now ...

I rather watch the smoke
escaping like a sigh.
Let it twist and rise
slipping through my fingers.
I don't know why,
but I need something
cleansing tonight.

Capture Them Quick

I wonder when things come to mind
is it my inspiration or does something else coincide?

Were these images lent to me?
A story from someone else's lips?
When to my life they have no connection,
yet still the thoughts they do drip ...

into my conscious, faces, and names
I have never known.
Perhaps I saw them that one day ...
I couldn't identify even with their picture shown.

Yet, why do they seem
so perfectly vivid in my dreams?
then from there to paper,
wasting hundreds of reams.
Just off of how I see them
what my imagination deems
Worthy
but it is all topsy turvy.

It should not matter,
yet my muse screams and shouts
I would never dare combat her
my confidence now in tatters.

Writer's block and
fears of the blank page
enough to tip my worst of moods
into despair and worthless rage.

Capture them quick
before they fade
running as fast as they can
like they want to get away,

but then why visit me at all?
What is the point
when out of the hole I finally crawl?
Their story never told
in that thing I create
and finally in that telling
their worries I did satiate.

He Whispers

Can I creep inside your mind
for just a little while?
See what it is you hide
behind that lingering smile?

How far deep does this go?
Games? They've all been played.
It they'll never know.
Tear away that face.
A little illusion
just hiding in the shade.
I've realize truth does hide
in meadows of twilight
hidden from our sight.
Nothing is truly right
yet you keep on
smiling;
curling up your lips
triggering our doubt.
My finger it was on it,
but it so quickly fades.
Who is on our side?

Can I creep inside your mind?
What the point
If a game can't be played?
Answer me,
is there any reason for you to stay?

Compromise

Compromise?
What is there to compromise about?
As I popped those seeds into my mouth
I decided both would only do

Husband,
Mother,
Love me if you can't love one another.

Why should I choose?
Why should I conform to you?
I want both.
I want flow.
I want Death and
Life.

I won't give up my flowers for a crown.
This throne is still is still mine
as I move above ground.

Compromise?
What is there to compromise about?
Sovereign in my own
decisions:
to love the growth and decay to bone
embodying it all,
rise and fall,
cycle through
my love
my life.

I choose my own route.
So tell me
what is there
to compromise about?

A Letter For Sobek

I think he wants me in the mud.
I thinks he wants me to devour
myself
instead of keeping this all nicely aligned
up on a shelf.

When mold grows over ink
it is hard to remember it's okay to sink
into the muck.
Eat me alive.
Violence isn't always something to strive
against.

I think I'm tired of guessing,
of searching for other meaning
through haze confusion,
my dreams reeling.

What is just out of reach?
How do you hold her so gently between your teeth?
You've torn my flesh
and pulled me in tight,
yet the fear is not what is triggered by your might.

An old friend shakes his head
"This is more than
your experience has ever given."
26 was a number I thought he would be,
but 26 is now coming for me
and it feels like you: strong, sly, skulking

through muddy water.
Forget the dry cracked skin
scales hold all of that ancient power within.

So if you drown me,
eat me alive,
will I finally be able to see
the knowledge hidden
behind crocodile eyes?
Curiosity
seems to be my trait of mine.
Divinity satisfied and brought back
time after time

Your claws now in my veins ...
How is it I'm still in control of these reins,
grasped loosely in my own two hands?

Feet and fingers both bleed.
Inside of my own soul
you swim now
contently.

Change
Chaos
Crocodile
My trinity

This

I fixed this:
the broken pieces.
I fixed it
when life came crashing in,
when I lost my way,
when they led me astray,
when family and friends,
were all too broken to.

I found out that to
follow the plan
better go it alone.
I gather up the pieces
new and old
gave away and sold
so much.

I fixed myself.
I fixed the life I wanted,
but I'm still a little bit broken,
beautifully broken.
I fixed what I could
when inspiration was stolen

by despair,
not a care for where life was going.

Still, I'm sitting here
collaged up, fixed up
to something I actually like
when I look in mirror.
Oh dear...

I fixed this.
No.
I made this.
From life's scattered pieces.
I made this!
collaborate if you wish.
Here: look how pretty we can make this stitch.
I've heard some fill the crack with gold.
Boulder and boulder we will grow.
Proud as we
reap what we sow,
cozily admiring everything
we have foretold.

I made this:
Broken beautifully perfect.

Happiness Satisfied

Happiness,
Is it subtle content
or a energy surging
joy overflowing?
How will I know
the razor thin line
between a comforting breath of release
and settling for all the things,
afraid of disturbing the peace?

I speak words
hoping for a strong result
then afraid of the ground shifting
knowing it is my fault.
Better to have done
loved and lost,
yet I can't help
but over-think the cost
of falling just short.
How do you become
the fool again
when your naivety
hasn't always been your friend?
A leap of faith
to something great
or maybe satisfaction
is kept behind
my own garden gate.

Hi It's Me...

Hi…. it's me
Is this the right number?
Can you even hear me speaking?
Does the signal reach the underworld
you know, completely?

Can you hear me?
'Cause I'm a bit worried.
You always handle me so gently,
Your presence: change and contentment
comforting contradictions
leave me glowing.

Hi, it's me
and I don't really understand...
There are flowers and rain and wind
everywhere in this new land.
Every breath is relief.
Even my sadness is so shallow
it barely can even seep
into my bones,
the place already taken by the cold.

Hi, it's me
Remember when you grabbed me?
your eyes changed color so rapidly
and that smell was there lingering
wouldn't leave me alone for weeks.
Were you as fascinated
by your first steps beneath

death?
Did it take your breath away?
Change your beliefs?

Hi, it's me
I know my messages just keep coming,
but normally I get a small sign
a vision, at least a little something
to know when you are coming
back around.
This other divine
presence is the only one
making any sound.
He's fine.
I'm fine,
I swear.
But that doesn't mean
I don't still wish you were here.

Hi, it's me
Wherever you are I hope it is fulfilling
with seeds of knowledge bursting,
sweet juice flowing over your lips
to water those flowers
that twist around your fingers
legs, hips, and wrist.
I wish I could say
Your silence isn't deafening.

Hi, it's me
Patience is a trait that escapes me.
I know maybe I should be so demanding of divinity,
but how do I keeping heading down this path
without your guiding hands and smile?
It would be so nice to hear from you
even just the shortest while.

Hi, It's me
Hello?
Are you there?
Persephone?

In Due Time

It has been so long
since I could linger in peace.
The memory is fading oh so quickly
all fogged over a dream
instead of anything close
to my previous reality.

Yet here I feel the clock slowly counting down
even the seconds seem to pause
and what is missing is the sound
of rushing panic.
What else did I forget?
What did I misplace?
Where else did I miss my target?

What should I curate
to banish this feeling of hate?
It surrounds me
suddenly it's gone and then
peace, quiet, serenity.
A moment to breath
visits me everyday
and smiles at me so pleasantly.

I'm tense as I shake their hand.
I feel my shoulders refusing to bend
at my commands.
I know it will take
more time to realize
the pauses in between seconds

are here to stay.
A true gift from something divine.
All in due time
when my mind, soul, and body
can all coincide
the habit of knowing
we have found what we wanted;
our happiness realized.

I Use To Hate Spring

I use to Hate spring
a needless stop to summer,
but now I know it means
You are returning

Hello Spring,
With your bit of warmth
little chill in the wind,
maybe it's a gift from death
to remind us
of where we have been.

It is light then dark
and most likely wet.
All the colors seem brand new
even though I did not forget

Thank you Spring.
You keep the wheel spinning.
I know her hand is responsible
for its constant turning.

I know she has love waiting
underneath all this life
someone waiting for the return
of his ever changing wife.

Hello Spring.
Thank you for all this green.
Chills in her arms

and warmth in her eyes.
Oh, how I've missed my matron
and her ever constant
surprise.

I Think It Is Meant To Be

It's breath it's green
I think it is meant to be.
Worst days are over
singing in my head
gray gloom and first blooms,
refreshing of the dead.

I think about you still ...
how you never loved me
and never will
and I smile knowing
who she was:
the one you chased and tossed away
was never really me,
at least no longer today.

She was mid breaking point
confused, lost and distraught.
I'm amazed at how I can
kinda look the same,
yet there is a different person in me
and I'm playing a different game.

The foolish is now only fun.
The mischief has just begun.
Commit to your mistakes,
acknowledging every time I have been fake
instead of true,
too enthralled by the thought of you
only then to remember all my agreements.
It will only confuse.

It is breath.
It is green.
I think it is meant to be:
me being here and for once
not really hating anything.

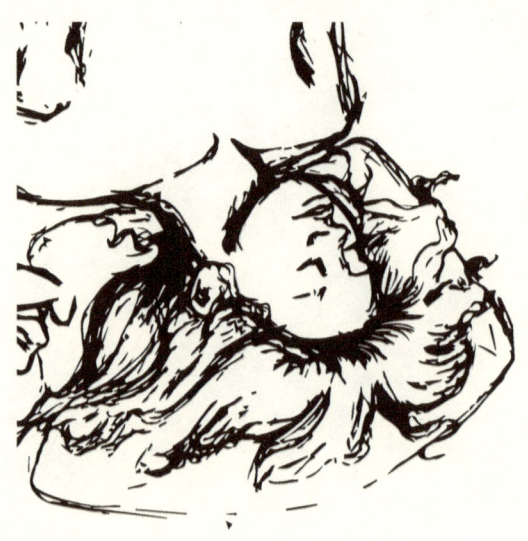

Into Them We Fall

What is this place
beyond our imagine state
where strange things lie
yet somehow we still relate?

When physics is defied
in the lies we do abide
and all the facts and truths
slip and slide.

We wander there with the sun
beaming in our face.
We can jump in and out
all evidence of our journey
gone without a trace.

Yet effects linger
when odd images and words take their grip
from our daily tasks to them
our minds will forever slip
till we give meaning
to their constant repeating,
hoping reason will start gleaming
between the fog and cracks of what
we keep seeing.

If they never mattered
why do we have them at all?
Why in both day and night
into our dreams do we fall?

It Comes In Tides

Magick comes and goes in tides
never entirely satisfied.
Run Hide
forget the meaning
light hidden in their eyes.

I'd rather run through the rain.
See the escape plan,
tear it up,
take a stand,
see if it is worth
reaching out my hand.

Resist the itch.
Axe can fall a little too quick.
Pull away:
pain or gain?
Both intertwined
If you're to stay sane.
It's the feeling of it
in my grasp
not what is hidden,
strong and defended,
all behind a latch.

Iron cold taste
in my mouth.
Entertain the demons
like dear old Faust.

A soul to trade?
Darling, it is your mistake.
Hearts are kept
while the love does freely bleed.
Intercept my logic's reason.
My curiosity is oh so hungry.
It will need to feed.

Shadows

I'm not afraid of the shadows
because I know where the light goes;
I know how to shift and move
and watch the glisten and flow.

I know of the blood and cells
that surround my bones
inside with no light
still my body continues to move and grow.

It is all unknown
till curiosity makes the pain
easy to move past,
more intrigued by the gain
of knowledge as I feel around
in the dark
and then the surroundings
feel apart
of me
not some foreign thing.
An unknown entity.

It's Frustration

It's frustration
wondering if their stares are admirations
or contempt.

Can they sense the desire within,
that you're not here
not yet
'cause I'm caught
craving instant gratifying
sensations.

Been so long since I felt the touch
but without that love would it be enough,
or send me into spirals
downward troubles?

Once upon a time
I used to be fucked just right
till hearts found pieces too loose not tight.
Limbo I have found
knowing that if it's not a spark
it'll be black and white.
If my breath won't catch
then it'll be regret,
but I've had a taste.
It is not something to forget.

With ease I slip in:
Lonely
Encasing
Craving.
It's all so frustrating.

Fingers On The Spine

They tell me I shouldn't be waiting
with bated breath.
I should be living,
enjoying each moment as they come to pass.
But how do you enjoy a book
without even opening the first page?

I haven't even seen the cover,
just let my fingers roll down the spine
with an aggravated sigh
my breath escapes.

I wonder if anyone else has felt this?
A knowing in their bones.
I was never incomplete,
yet feel both empty and whole,
didn't yet belong
always looking out the window,
reading into the subtext of every song,
searching the eye of every person I met
and knowing the feeling of wrong,
looking for one I haven't even met.

But is that really true?
Maybe this life made me forget?
Forget your eyes
Your hair
Your smell
Your face
All faded and warbled
in dreams fogged over
out of place.

That voice use to be as clear as the music in my ears.
Now that too has faded with all these years.

Still I sense you are close
all cells on high alert,
each one I meet feeling a step closer.
I can never really be sure.

"Stop worrying," they say,
"stop searching just be.
Live your life!"
is all they seem to scream.
But how can I understand a story
that I haven't had a chance to read?

Rebuilding

I destroyed it,
ripped it all to shreds.
Now, standing in this rubble
I'm afraid I want it back.

Though I know the destruction had its purpose
those shallow feelings don't deserve us.
Rebuild a different path.
What's so wrong with looking back
on fractured memories
all so incomplete and tantalizing?
That hurt now feels so friendly.
Have to remind myself
all this repetition breeds
insanity.

Is it just the growing pain
searching for the comfort of structure,
snuggling into feeling the same
routine and even forever held dreams.
Rebuild and pull from
what I once thought was only make believe.

What is next?
Step by step
bridges all burned down
and I know I did it.
Sinister lingerings hold so strong
even though I feel this peace,
wondering if I finally belong.

Cliches fly around,
but is it because their sounds
ring oh so true.
Will I feel this all over again
when I finally find you?

In the Middle Of July

Why is it always
in the middle of July
when anxiety seems to get the best of me?

Is it summer silence
pacing trying to remember my triumphs,
slipping into habitual thoughtful violence.

Some days I keep hold
of bad memories.
All the things you once meant to me
slowly picking them out
like crumbs stuck in between my teeth

I still beat my knuckles against
the steering wheel like you use to.
Is there something about me like that
that you still cling to?
Like me do you hate yourself
a little bit more
when the feeling takes over
and you kick down the door?

Let me linger in good feeling of bad times.
Let me remember the pain of my heart
as your hand took mine.
Take me back to burning your letters
and hating the month of July
as I slowly realized
all the past years
was just a pack of lies.

I wish I didn't emulate you
and that it didn't feel good to.
I wish those that I sit across from
didn't look anything like you.

I'm probably nothing to your grand scheme
and I'm holding on to my last breath that
you'll be the same to me.

Just the taste test
before I finally get the real thing.

Capricorn Horns Tell Me

Slip? Drip?
Get a grip.
Plan it out.
Figure it out.
The horns did warn you
ground the sound
of all the thoughts in your head.
I swear
nothing is there,
just the voices in your head.

Release
the tease.
Freeze the peace.
Forget your needs.
Produce.
Abuse
and always refuse
all that does not
reciprocate.

Your fate
is locked behind the garden gate.
Punctual.
Fixate on all that
Love
had to dominate.

It's fine.
Toe the line.
Breathe for a
second of release.
Keys:
Missing.
Do you dare please?
Pity watching
you walking.
Your feet occasionally stomping.

What?
Tough stuff!
Forget the meaning of.
Balance what you replace.
This is what you do
'cause life is just
too fucking strange.

Stuck In A Pause

Stuck in a pause.
A hunt in my blood
sharpening ridiculous
claws.

A face is present
hidden behind my vision
making me incapable
of simple decisions,

reminded with stories
of feelings I've lost
returning so quickly
and that is the pause.

Hesitant feeling of
fingers on my skin.
No hand is there,
but I can't help but compare.

I search for the marks.
Reminder lingering
of too real thoughts.
I remember reality,
but no effect
does it's laws
seem to have on this
comforted feeling
waiting in my chest.

Heart beat
like the clock is ticking;
the alarm hasn't gone off yet.

Just lay there half asleep
knowing soon a feeling complete
consumed by delectable treat.

Features all there,
but there is smoke in the air
clouding my clarity
quite simply not fair.

It's an antique
this critique
of my trusting beliefs.
Overriding the logic
they are claiming their seat.

I'm too afraid.
I'm not yet complete
or maybe it doesn't matter
and I haven't admitted defeat.

I'm stuck in a pause
ruminating its cause.
A half step away from
where you wait:
a slow clap
my heart
thundering applause.

Will You Welcome Me?

Hello moss covered graves.
Some of your names have worn away.
It is oh so humid here.
I was wondering if you could lend a ear?

What was it like to die
in a place like this?
Did you feel its magick
or feel it was amiss?
Did you wish for love,
adventure, ever after, something more?
Did you feel neglected?
End this life rich or poor?
Did that even matter
as death opened its door?

I hope we're not intruding,
my sister and I,
but something drew us to you
even as a storm hovers in the sky.

We read these names
carved in your graves
hoping to know you,
feel into the depth of this sacred place.

Some of you fell over,
some were tended well,
some are so worn
who you were we could never tell.

It's a mix of feelings
as we turn to leave.
This last question I must ask:
when it's my own time
will you welcome me?

For I feel here,
with moss covered graves,
I could rest easy
when it is the end of my days.

Who ever you are
please never stop searching for your own
little piece of magic.

Samantha Nicole Traina currently resides in Portland Oregon where she is finding her magick with witchcraft, art, and the rest of life. For even more of her creative content check out her Youtube channel Shadow Harvest or her podcast Coffee and Cauldrons.

Social Media
Instagram: @Shadowharvest
Twitter: @Shadowharvestw
Website: ShadowHarvestWitch.com